Buried

Treasure

By Selma Cook

Many of the events and situations in this book were experienced by either the author herself or people who are close to the author. To protect the privacy of certain individuals, the names and identifying details have been changed.

Author: Selma Cook

ISBN 978-0-6458463-1-7 (Paperback)

ISBN 978-0-6458463-2-4 (E-book)

A Catalog record for this book is available from the National Library of Australia

Foreword

When I met Selma Cook, she had just started working on the book *'Buried Treasure'*. At first, I thought it was a book based on hunting for treasure. However, to my surprise, when I read it, I discovered that the 'treasure' is in fact spiritual treasure, not material treasure.

The Amirah Stevenson series is about the journey, and often humorous adventures, of a small Muslim family from Australia. Amirah is on the threshold of adolescence, and faced with life's complexities has only her father and spritely grandmother to turn to for advice.

This wonderful series is especially pertinent to Muslim teenagers who are thrown off balance by the many challenges in today's world. It is foremost for adolescents who are searching for meaning and understanding, and who struggle to maintain a balance between such influences and their commitment to their very special religion.

Naseema Mall

Journalist, South Africa

Dedication

To my children and my children's children, whose dreams awaken me and whose smiles lift my heart.

CHAPTER 1

Granny

Amirah walked down the street from school towards her Granny's house. Something she had done for a few years now, since she had declared she was big enough to walk the few streets alone. Granny had let her walk the short distance, always eager to instill confidence in her. Amirah took long strides, lifting her feet as she walked, moving easily and quietly.

She gazed around as she strolled, looking at the passing cars, smiling at the antics of birds clambering over some leftover crumbs, watching huge trees swaying their branches in the breeze and the cloudy sky that threatened rain. She could smell the humidity thick in the air. She quickened her step.

Thoughts floated in the back of her mind, some troubling her. The ever-present gap in her heart that her mother's death had left her with. Her mother. Her mum. Someone she had never really known. Someone she would never know. Someone she needed to know. In her waking dreams she pictured her as a tall, graceful woman, always wanting to be with her, lifting her high in the air, absorbed in her childish giggles. A woman enshrouded with light, a silhouette in her mind's eye of all that is beautiful. Of all that is good.

But at times like today, the thought of her mum took on a troubling hue, representing a cycle of grief that she had known since the age of three. Images of beauty, happiness, delight. Followed by feelings of loss, sadness, and the inevitable loneliness and searching. Thoughts of what could have been, what might have been and what are. A cycle.

Other thoughts poked at her, demanding her attention. Worrying taunts from the bullies in her class who had taken up her dad as a figure of ridicule. She frowned at the thought. They taunted her, but from a distance because beneath the calm exterior of this year seven student, was a strong and vibrant spirit. Despite her sense of loss and the inner exertions of growing up and finding her place in the world, Amirah exhibited the strength and confidence that comes from knowing that she is loved.

She turned the corner into Granny's street and skimmed her hands over the tops of the picket fences and bushy hedges as she hurried along. She quickened her gait when she saw the bright red bougainvillea that had spread across the front of the house, creating a natural archway as she approached the side gate.

※

The branches of the willow tree brushed against Granny's kitchen window making little scraping sounds like fingernails on a blackboard.

The wind was beginning to blow, and the skies darkened. The old lady paused in her reading of the newspaper to peer over the top of her spectacles at the green leaves and threatening storm that disturbed her winter day's quiet time at the kitchen table. She smiled to herself, glanced at the clock, and started reading again.

After a few minutes she could hear something else that rose distinctly from the sound of the howling wind and Granny recognized the eager footsteps instantly. Gingerly, she folded her newspaper and sat back in her chair with her arms crossed in front of her, waiting for the inevitable knock at the outside door. Sure enough, a short time later a rather hurried rat-a-tat-tat could be heard from beyond the unlocked back door that opened onto the porch.

"Come on in my dear," called out Granny. "The door isn't locked." Granny smiled.

Amirah fumbled. Juggling school bag and jacket, which she abandoned, along with her shoes, she entered the porch. Finally, she succeeded in undoing the old, rusty latch. She opened it, then gently closed it again with a decisive click. She padded quietly across the mat glancing at the pot plants and vines growing into every crevice of the little glassed-in porch. Amirah brushed aside some straggling vines to open the back door and enter the cozy kitchen.

"*As salam alaikum* Granny!" called out Amirah with a distinctive smile. Her tall slender frame brought perspective to the little kitchen, giving it an air of childish playfulness and joy.

"*Wa alaikum salam* Princess," responded Granny with a smile that made the tiny wrinkles around her eyes bunch up together, forming an array of tidy lines framing her face.

"You must be cold my dear. Come and sit down here next to the heater and I'll make you a warm drink."

Granny fussed. She drew Amirah's chair closer to the heater and obediently Amirah sat down on the cushioned kitchen chair, rubbing her hands together and blowing on them with steamy breath.

"So, how's things Granny?" asked Amirah.

"Just fine. Just fine, *Alhamdulillah*. And what about you?"

"Oh, just the same."

The cloudy thoughts that had followed Amirah as she walked to Granny's house reappeared, settling on her, reflected on her face.

Granny looked at the young girl out of the corner of her eye as she placed the shiny teapot on the stove. Her fingers shook ever so slightly as she lit the match. Whenever she detected that something was amiss with Amirah, she had a feeling of helplessness along with an ardent desire to help, to comfort, to fill in the gaps that she knew she could never fill.

"How's school dear?"

"Okay," said Amirah.

She smiled as she watched Granny moving around her kitchen.

"And your dad?"

"Busy."

Granny didn't interrogate her any more than that. She took down two rather large coffee mugs from the shelf above the sink and popped a tea bag in each.

Amirah looked at her Granny and at the kitchen with its shiny kettle and carefully arranged cups on the shelf. This place had always made her feel safe.

"You know Granny, I think you've got the tidiest kitchen in the world. It looks like something out of a magazine."

"How nice of you to say so," said Granny, with a little twinkle in her eyes.

"I heard that tidy people have well organized brains," observed Amirah, staring at Granny with a raised eyebrow.

"Well, that could be right, or it could be that the individual would like to have an organized brain but failed, so tidied her kitchen instead!"

Granny laughed out loud.

"Oh, I think you're pretty organized upstairs Granny," noted Amirah, smiling as she pointed to her head. She loved to joke with Granny.

"Yes, I must say, kitchens aside, I don't miss much dear, including the fact that you have something on your mind."

"Well, it's Dad."

"Really? What's wrong?" Granny sat down next to Amirah, sipping her tea, and listening intently.

"He's just busy all the time and I don't get to see him much."

"It's not easy working freelance dear. He must take the work when it comes and you know he loves you to bits and pieces, so don't worry." Granny leaned forward and spoke directly into Amirah's gaze. Her old green eyes saw the loneliness in those deep blue eyes.

"I know that Granny, and I really don't want to be selfish but sometimes I need to talk to him, and he just sits in front of the computer and nods his head and says a word now and then to let me think he is listening."

"Listen my dear, if your dad is busy and you want to talk – about anything – anything at all – you can come over here and talk to me – whenever you want, just like you've always done."

Granny patted Amirah's hand and gave it a little squeeze.

"I've known you since you were born. Small and cute and squirming in my arms and I took care of your mum when she was ill all those years ago. I think I know you well young lady and you must know that you can talk to me about anything. Okay?"

"I know Granny and I do."

"Do what dear?"

"I do talk to you. Well, here I am, right?"

"And on such a lovely day!" exclaimed Granny.

"It's cloudy and looks like it will rain *cats and dogs* out there!" cried Amirah.

"Don't you just love it? There is something so exceptionally beautiful about the garden after a good rain. I love the smell of it."

"I usually just feel wet in the rain Granny."

"That's because you still haven't learned to see the beauty that's around you. But *Inshaa Allah* you will when you grow up a bit."

Granny gazed out the window. It had started to rain heavily, and the trees were swaying from side to side.

"Granny."

"Yes."

"I don't have many friends at school, you know."

"Really?"

"Yeah. The kids call me 'snowball' and say I'm from the Arctic and call me 'Viking' and all that."

"They're probably jealous."

"Of what Granny?"

"You'd be surprised what people get jealous about dear. You just never know what is going on inside people's heads. And by the way, your family is from Europe and there is nothing wrong with that."

"But I was born in Australia, so why all the talk about Vikings and the Arctic? Like I live in an igloo near polar bears!"

"I really don't know the answer to that. But I do know that sometimes people like to think they're better than others. It might have something to do with skin colour, or facial features, language or dress, a million different things. But look, everyone has their beauty – whether inside or out – and sometimes both. Just accept the way you are and be the best you can be."

"Thanks Granny."

Amirah paused.

"The kids say I've got a long nose and call me '*squeagle beak*'!"

"*Squeagle beak*! That's a new one. *Squeagle beak*, really? I don't know what to say!"

Granny studied Amirah's nose.

"It seems fine to me, dear. Just laugh it off. You know, people often say nasty things because they want to see how you'll react but if you don't care about what they say, they soon give up. Mark my words, the kids at school used to call me all sorts of names and that's what my mum told me."

"Okay Granny. I'll try to laugh it off."

Amirah wasn't convinced. She smiled and touched her nose.

"Do I have a long nose Granny?"

Amirah turned her head and stared up at the ceiling, hoping that Granny could then have a close look at her nose. Granny sat forward and inspected Amirah's nose from various angles.

"You have a lovely nose my darling and don't worry, I grew into mine."

"Really. Did you have a long nose when you were my age?"

"Put it this way, my nose grew first, and I caught up later."

Granny laughed out loud and winked at Amirah.

"And you know what else? All those nasty little girls who called me names probably don't have a cozy kitchen or a wonderful granddaughter like me! Life catches up with people."

Granny smiled as she gazed around her.

"It goes a bit deeper than just my nose Granny," said Amirah, sitting up straight in her chair and taking a deep breath.

"What else do they say?" asked Granny, putting down her cup of tea.

"Some kids say things about dad, and well, try to make him look silly."

"Oh, do they?" asked Granny, frowning.

"It hurts me when they say things about him. The other day, Granny, I punched a girl."

"You didn't!"

"Oh, yes I did!"

"That's probably exactly what those nasty little wretches wanted you to do, and you fell for it. Keep your dignity my dear and ignore them."

"It's too hard. I can't."

"What do they say about Adam?" asked Granny.

"All kinds of karate names and road runner and silly things like that."

"He can certainly run, that's for sure," commented Granny.

Granny sipped at her tea again.

"Listen my sweet girl, you have a very special dad and don't let anyone change your opinion. People can say whatever they like but they can't change the reality."

"What is the reality Granny? Dad doesn't talk to me. At least, not about important things. I see him training and I love to watch him, and he and I have a lot of fun, but sometimes it's like there is a wall between us. He just never, never talks about Mum, and I'm bursting like I will explode."

By this time Amirah had got off her chair and was waving her arms, punctuating each sentence with a gesture of her hands. Granny looked at Amirah and sighed.

"Have you tried to bring the subject up?"

"A number of times but when I get close to the subject, he just excuses himself and the next thing I know he's off running somewhere."

Amirah was clearly exasperated.

Granny stared at a spot on the tablecloth for a few moments. Her gaze became dazed, and she shook her head a little to clear her vision. Amirah sat in silence, moody over the subject that seemed to bear no fruit.

"Will you talk to me about my Mum? Will you Granny?"

Her eyes were pleading.

"Of course, dear. Ask me whatever you want."

"I know I was only three when she died and that was nine years ago. I really don't remember so much, just a few flash backs. I remember feeling warm and safe. I remember playing at her feet and the shape of her eyes, but I can't remember what her face looked like."

Amirah was using her hands to describe her memories and Granny sat and watched her.

"If you want to see what your mum looked like when she was twelve years old, just go and have a look in the mirror."

Amirah was surprised.

"You mean I look like Mum? People always say I resemble Dad."

"Oh, they just say that. They don't want to remind him of her. He misses her terribly."

"I know."

"Be patient and keep asking Allah. The chance will come for you to talk to him, and things will be better. It takes time for people to heal."

Granny paused.

"Your dad is a good man. I'm sure his faith has kept him going all these years. Everyone has their own personal struggle, and this is his. So, try to help him with it and if you need to talk, come to old Granny. Okay?"

Amirah nodded.

"I'm so glad you understand Granny. If you didn't, I don't know what I would do!"

"Now, come on. Families help each other! *Alhumdulilah* we have each other!"

Granny smiled warmly, then she got up from the table and put the cups in the sink.

"I can't believe you hit a girl at school Amirah. I just can't imagine you doing it," commented Granny, puzzled.

"Well, of course, you know that Dad has taught me self-defense since I could walk. I did it without thinking. I never meant to hurt her. I just wanted to make her stop!"

"Yes, I know dear," said Granny knowingly. "Show me something of what you know."

"Okay," said Amirah, getting off her chair and turning her back on the old lady.

"Now you just come up behind me and act like you're going to attack me," suggested Amirah.

Granny wiped her hands on her apron and started to walk like a gangster in the street. She was moving her arms widely as she walked, pretending to shine her knuckle busters on the sleeve of her jacket. Amirah could see her out of the corner of her eye and laughed.

"Cool Granny. You just need some piercings and tattoos, and I would be seriously afraid of you!" laughed Amirah.

"Just watch it lovey," said Granny, trying to sound like a tough guy. And then she swung round and pinned Amirah's arms behind her tightly.

"Hey sweet 'art, your money or your life!"

Amirah ducked, turned and a few short seconds later, she had 'Bikey Granny' in a very gentle headlock.

"How's that Gran?"

"Oh, that's good dear, very good. Can you let me go? Please. I promise I'll never beat up anyone again. Okay!"

Amirah released Granny and helped her straighten her hair. Granny rearranged her spectacles and took a closer look at Amirah.

"You're pretty good for a kid, Princess. Those little wretches at school had better watch it, huh?"

Granny's face was quite red, but her shiny silver hair hardly appeared out of place.

"But before you think you're too good for yourself, just have a look at this." Without another word, Granny scooped up Amirah and had her on the floor with her arms pinned behind her and was tickling her as she pulled her scarf over her eyes. Then she started pulling her ears. As hard as she tried, Amirah could not get out of Granny's hold.

"Okay Granny, you win. I know you're the champ. I give up."

Amirah could hardly talk for laughing. They both ended up sitting on the kitchen floor with Granny wiping the tears from her eyes.

"Who'd have thought that a sweet little girl like you could put a poor helpless old lady like me in a headlock!"

And off they went again, laughing until Amirah's sides ached.

CHAPTER 2

Bridges

Amirah and her father lived in a small house near the city center. They didn't really like the busy crowded atmosphere of the inner suburbs, but it was much more convenient for her father's work.

Besides, Granny lived quite close by. After Amirah's mother died, they had left the outer suburbs to be near the publishing houses and newspaper offices where her father sold his writing. The time it took him to travel from the city to home was just more time away from his 'Princess'. So, now Amirah went to a girl's school within walking distance of her house.

Amirah gazed around the kitchen and remembered Granny's neat and tidy cupboards and shelves and sighed. She hitched up her apron and started rummaging through the cupboard looking for a sieve.

Sure enough, at half past five there was a click in the lock and the handle turned slowly. The door opened with hardly a sound and Amirah sat on the sofa waiting for her father to enter the room. She could hear him in the hallway. By now he would have slipped off his comfy trainers, put his briefcase on the hall table and hung his sheepskin jacket on the hall stand.

A cheery face appeared in the doorway of the living room. Curly blonde hair fell haphazardly over his eyes and his ginger beard was shining with drops of rainwater. Deep blue eyes fell upon Amirah as she sat smiling on the sofa, and his very straight, not-too-long nose peeked out from between his tousled hair and shiny beard. Amirah took a close look at his nose.

"Hmm, I must have got Mum's nose," she thought.

She smiled.

"*As salam alaikum* Dad. You look like a wreck," commented Amirah playfully.

"*Wa alaikum assalam* Princess. I got caught in a storm. Can't you tell?" he joked. "I'll just go and clean up. Is dinner ready?"

"Almost," replied Amirah.

She jumped up and took the green salad from the fridge and then heated up the spaghetti sauce. She put a load of pasta onto two plates and poured the sauce into a glass bowl. The little kitchen table was prettily decorated with a checked tablecloth, salt and pepper shakers shaped like pineapples and a small vase of daisies.

It wasn't too long before Adam entered the room at a steady gait and plonked himself down onto the floor in front of his dinner. Sitting comfortably on cushions, they started to eat.

"This tastes so nice, *Mashallah*," commented her dad, "but then I am starving."

He winked at her.

"I know it tastes good. I followed the recipe step by step."

"Now, that's what I like about you! Methodical and sure of yourself."

"I'm not really Dad."

"Not really what?"

"Sure of myself."

She wondered if she should continue.

"In fact, there seems to be so many things I'm unsure of."

"Wow. Where did that come from?" he thought.

Adam looked at her, his gaze leaving his dinner for just a few short seconds.

"Unsure of what?" Adam had stopped what he was doing.

"Of myself and who I am. I am growing up Dad. Didn't you notice?"

"Yeah, oh yeah, of course I do. Can't help it really. You're getting really tall and well, kind of becoming the lady of the house, I guess." Adam wasn't sure what to say.

Amirah watched him as he settled down to eat again. A few lines were drawn on her forehead. She wanted to say something and didn't quite know how to begin. In this situation it would be difficult for him to get up and go for a run. Maybe it was the right time.

"If you don't mind Dad, I'd really like to ask you about Mum."

Before he could reply, she added, "I know you don't like talking about the whole thing and I do understand but Dad, you know, we must talk. It is really so very important to me."

She looked at him beseechingly and he held her gaze for what seemed a long time. His hand had paused between his plate and his mouth.

"Sorry Princess. I know I've been – well - evasive."

His words stumbled out and he was obviously nervous. Amirah was sorry she had brought up the subject. Maybe it was just the wrong time again.

"Granny spoke to me today," he added with a smile. "Well, spoke is not the right word perhaps," he said, smiling more broadly. "You know, my Mum has quite a way of convincing people."

He rubbed his ears meaningfully as he spoke.

"I have a surprise for you. In fact, I was going to tell you after dinner, but I may as well tell you now."

Amirah was surprised.

"What could it be?" she thought to herself.

Feeling excited, she waited for him to speak.

"I thought we could take a couple of days and head down to The Retreat. I think we both could do with a change. What do you reckon?" asked Adam with a twinkle in his eye that gave Amirah a sudden gush of hope.

"Absolutely! Great, Dad! When are we going?"

"As soon as we clean up these dishes and get ready."

Dinner was over quickly, and Adam washed up the dishes while Amirah prepared a box of food to take with them.

"What did you put in that box?" he asked curiously.

"Just a few necessities of life," said Amirah, grinning.

"Like?"

"Instant noodles, corn flakes and Weetbix, your rye bread, chocolate, butter and vegemite."

"Any real food?"

"Don't worry Dad, I'm just going to put your bean shoots and that green stuff in a container."

"Make sure you put enough for two," he said.

Amirah obediently filled a container with carrots, lettuce, bean shoots, zucchini and fresh ripe tomatoes.

"There are some lamb chops in the freezer, you can wrap them in newspaper, and they'll be thawed out by tomorrow. We can have them for dinner *Inshaa Allah*, with the green stuff."

As he spoke, the kitchen was put into place. He took off the apron he always wore on such occasions, and tousled Amirah's hair.

"Don't worry, everything will be all right." He turned her around and stared at her straight in the eyes.

"You're not the only one making *du'aa* that all this will turn into something good," he said.

The twinkle in his eye was gone and a serious look clouded his gentle face. "I know that Allah has only to say the word 'Be' and whatever He wills will happen. We must ask, do our best and trust in Him."

Amirah nodded her head. She didn't understand exactly what he meant but she had a very sure feeling that soon she would.

"Dad."

"Yes."

"Will we take Granny with us this time?"

"Not this time."

"Why?" asked Amirah.

"Well, she told me about your fighting ability today and said she might accidently upset you and then she'd be in trouble again, so perhaps it was better she stays in town."

Amirah laughed along with her dad.

"So, she told you about the headlock, huh?"

"Yes, and I might add that she was quite impressed. Want to try it out on me?" he asked challengingly.

"Me? You? Never!"

Amirah backed away from him, laughing.

"You're the champ Dad and remember, like you always told me, never get into a fight that you know you can't win."

"Exactly. So that's why you tackled Granny?" he laughed again, knowing that Granny had got the best of Amirah.

"This time I underestimated my opponent."

"You sure did. Let me tell you something. It was Granny who taught me self-defense when I was *knee high to a grasshopper*!"

"Granny? Self-defense?"

"In her day, she was in competitions. Haven't you seen all those trophies? You know, the ones on the mantelpiece."

"Well, I did but I always thought they were yours or Grandpa's."

"Oh, I thought you were smart but ..."

This was certainly a day of surprises. By now Amirah and her dad were putting clothes into a bag, and blankets and pillows into striped zip bags.

"Granny a champion self-defense..." thought Amirah. "Why has she never told me about it?" she wondered.

Granny with her quiet demeanor, sharp tongue, and glorious sense of humour - well it seemed out of place. It didn't quite fit in with her knitting and all that.

"You know, I was only about seven when she became a Muslim, but I still remember her training and how she took me to my training every single day come rain or shine."

"You mean karate?" asked Amirah.

"No, in those days I did gymnastics. Didn't start karate till I was a bit older. Granny always said gymnastics prepares your body for anything."

"Was she right, Dad?" asked Amirah, as she folded another blanket.

"You'll find Princess, that Granny is usually right," he said with a laugh. "Come on, let's go. I think we're ready now."

Amirah ran through to her room and grabbed a few books. It was her favorite thing to sit huddled in a blanket on the rocks on the beach and read. Her eyes skimmed her bookshelf and her fingers tugged at two books. '*Life of the Final Messenger (peace be upon him)*' was one and the other was '*Guinness Book of Records*', new edition." She put them into her bag, closed the zipper, put on her jacket and scarf, and headed out the door.

CHAPTER 3

The Retreat

Amirah stirred in her sleep. The first soft rays of dawn peeped in her bedroom window and cast glimmering light on her cheeks. Its softness was accompanied by the steady crashing of waves that beat against the shore just a short distance from where she lay, snug and safe. There was, however, another kind of steady thud that made her open her eyes and concentrate on the sound. After a few seconds though, she settled back on her pillow.

"Dad's training," she smiled to herself.
Everything was normal; everything was fine.

She looked at her clock and sat up in bed, her feet reaching for her warm slippers. She slipped on her dressing gown and went to make *wudu'* and get ready to pray.

Adam heard her movement and called out, "*Assalam alaikum* sleepy head, I was just about to wake you up."

"Coming Dad, just give me a few minutes."

Amirah prayed in her room with the growing light shedding colors on the pale pink walls. When she finished, she walked quietly into the living room and saw her father, as usual, beating at the air with his hands and moving gracefully as he kicked his feet above his head and landed perfectly, with hardly a sound – a gentle thud – on the wooden floor.

"Don't you get tired, Dad?"

"What makes you ask that?" asked Adam, who was poised in the center of the living room, standing on one foot with his other foot resting comfortably against his knee. His arms were outstretched, and his eyes were closed in concentration. Slowly he raised himself onto his toes. Only his chest moved as he breathed slowly. There was no sound except the birds welcoming in the new day and the ever-crashing sound of waves.

"Well, you never seem tired," said Amirah, watching him with admiration. "You get up early and are on the go all day long."

"But I do sleep," he answered with a smile, still holding his position. "You have to respect your body then it will respect you," he added, "and I take good care of mine, *Alhamdulillah*."

"You sure do Dad," said Amirah. "By the way, can I ask you something?"

"Sure."

"Why do you like running so much?"

"I've always liked running," answered her dad. "Ever since I was a kid, I was always running."

Adam plopped onto the cushions on the floor and looked at Amirah. It was time to talk, he knew that. Something he had been dreading but he knew he had to, for her sake. He also knew that if he didn't open up to

Amirah and break down those barriers, his mother would tell him off! At the age of thirty-seven, he still had a healthy respect for his old mum.

"Were you running away from something?" asked Amirah.

"Yes. I was always getting beaten up at school."

"You're kidding! You! Beaten up! You must be joking Dad!"

Adam smiled.

"I was such a scrawny little kid with snow white hair and freckles. The kids used to call me 'snowball' and tell me to go back and live in an igloo!"

"No! Really Dad? Do you know the kids at school call me 'snowball' too?"

"So I hear," responded Adam. "Some things don't seem to change, do they?"

"When did you get so big, if you were a scrawny kid?"

"Not until I was about fifteen or so. That's why Mum, dear old Mum, put me into gymnastics and karate. She told me that there is nothing wrong with being little, but you can be little and strong. She dragged me screaming and yelling to my training every single day."

"Why were you screaming and yelling?"

"Training in gymnastics makes your muscles hurt, and sometimes it is scary. You know that."

"Is that all? I never squawk like that?"

Adam threw a cushion at her. "So, I was a bit of a wimp, but I grew out of it." Adam winked.

"Hmm. Did the kids stop beating you up?"

"Eventually."

"When you started karate?"

"Oh yes, by then they had."

"You used to beat them back?"

"Nope, never did."

"But there were many boys picking on you, weren't there?"

"Yes indeed. It was their idea of fun at lunch time to find 'snowball' and give him a hard time."

"Why didn't you run away?"

"I did! But they usually got me cornered."

"Tell me how they stopped."

Adam took a deep breath and sat back comfortably.

"My mum told me to ignore them, which I tried but found it hard to do. In the end I was so scared."

"Didn't your mum go to the school and complain?"

"She said I had to fight my own battles."

"Wow. Granny was a tough mum."

"Still is," laughed Adam."

"Then what happened?"

"After I'd been learning karate for a while, I got pretty good at it and my body was strong. I hadn't realized how strong I'd become - I guess I was too busy running!"

Adam started to laugh so much that he had tears in his eyes as he remembered.

"One day I came home all bloody and crying and beaten up."

"Was your dad alive then?"

"No, he had died some time before that."

"And then?"

"Well, your Granny got mad with me!"

"With you! Why?"

"She told me I shouldn't have let them do that to me and if I didn't go back the next day and stop the boy who had hit me, I was going to be in trouble! Boy, was I scared!"

"Of who? The boy or Granny?"

"Granny of course!" replied Adam.

"Did Granny use to smack you, Dad?" asked Amirah, tentatively.

"Nope! Never!" replied Adam.

Amirah shook her head in amazement.

"Why didn't Granny help you to stop the problem? Like complain to the school." Amirah was confused.

"She knew more about my abilities than I did. She wanted me to believe in myself. Not believe in her ability to help me." Adam paused, waiting for it all to sink in.

He continued. "Anyway, that night I could hardly sleep. I kept tossing and turning, trying to imagine how I was going to stop that boy. He was huge. A real bully. Nasty little so and so."

"Then what Dad? Come on tell me everything!"

"Well, Granny had to physically throw me out of the house the next morning and she told me she would call the school in fifteen minutes to make sure I was there. She didn't give me any means to escape. I felt like I was on death row." Adam was by now lying back on the cushions. Amirah was sitting on the other side of the room on another cushion, watching him intently.

"I can't talk anymore Princess."

Amirah was stunned.

"Why Dad? What's the matter now?"

"I'm starving!"

He smiled and threw another cushion her way. He continued to wear a subtle smile on his face, as he watched her get up.

"Don't forget! I'm making dinner today, so you are making breakfast. We have a deal!" he added.

"Granny was right," said Amirah, half under her breath.

"What did she say this time?" grinned Adam.

Amirah stopped and said, "Well, Granny said that the way to a man's heart is through his stomach, and I suppose it is also the way to get him to talk!"

With that, she walked indignantly out of the room.

"Hey Dad," called out Amirah from the kitchen.

"Yes."

"Do you want healthy stuff or real food?"

"Trying to be funny huh Princess?" said Adam. "Bananas, grapes, apples and a few pears sound just fine."

"Are you sure that's enough?" asked Amirah, smiling, as she put a platter of fruit down on the floor between them.

"Looks okay? Aren't you hungry Princess?" asked Adam.

He picked up a banana and peeled it. It disappeared instantly.

"You're amazing Dad, *Mashaa Allah*. I've never ever seen anyone eat as much as you and not get fat. Bananas are fattening, you know?"

"Who told you that?" he scoffed. "Probably the guy who wants to sell you the chocolate biscuits and potato chips," said Adam, not waiting to hear the answer. "You just eat as much fruit and vegetables as you want, exercise well, take it easy with everything else you eat and you'll be fine, *Inshaa Allah*."

The pile of banana peels was becoming something of a small hill beside Adam, and Amirah chuckled.

"Dad. You know the kids at school call you names."

"They still picking on me?" laughed Adam. "Must be the kids of my old school mates."

He slapped himself on the knee and exclaimed, "Tell me, what do they call me now?"

"You won't like it."

"Try me."

"Road Runner."

Amirah raised an eyebrow and watched for her father's response.

"I guess that makes them a bunch of coyotes!"

The room rang with his laughter. It was a few minutes before he could talk. Amirah found herself laughing too, although until that moment that name had always hurt her.

"How can you laugh at people calling you names? It's awful!" she said, between giggles.

"It's not that bad. Could have been heaps worse. I'd love to run like the Road Runner. Maybe I wouldn't have to write anymore!" His face shone.

"Okay Dad. You've eaten now, so can you tell me the rest of the story between you and that nasty kid?"

"Oh that. Okay. On that particular day, after Granny had finally managed to get me to school, I kept around the back of the shelter sheds hoping no one would see me. My face was red, and a bit swollen here and there, and I had a great big black eye. I'd skinned both my knees and altogether I was a sorry sight. I thought that if I kept away from everyone until the bell rang, I'd be Okay. Wrong."

"Yeah, and then?"

Amirah was leaning forward, hugging her knees. She looked like she was watching a film.

"From the corner of the shelter shed, I could see the kids lining up to go into the classroom and I was just about to make my dash and join the end of the line when I heard a voice behind me. It was that nasty kid. He said, 'Hey snowball.' My blood ran cold. I froze. I was so nervous and had so much pent-up emotion inside me that I thought I was going to burst. I turned and looked at him and he was laughing."

"Revolting kid," said Amirah, frowning.

"There were about five meters between me and him and he had his gang behind him."

"Coward!" declared Amirah indignantly.

"I wasn't going to wait for them to lay into me again and I was thinking about what Granny would say when I got home. I remember that I closed my eyes and asked Allah to help me. I was so afraid. I don't know how to tell you about the butterflies in my stomach and all that. Anyway, I just let loose and started kicking in the air, punching out and turning around. Just like a full-on training session. I had no idea what I was doing. Hadn't planned a thing. I think somewhere between it all I did a back flip and a couple of somersaults. It's a wonder they didn't all die laughing."

Amirah started to giggle. Adam was sitting up straight now demonstrating his moves and banana peels started flying over towards Amirah, but she ducked just in time and not even one got her.

"After I'd finished my little 'bonkers session' as the kids referred to it later, I just stood there feeling exhausted and trying not to cry."

"Sorry Dad, but you were a bit of a wimp."

"Anyway," said Adam, as another banana peel caught Amirah on the nose. "Don't be cheeky now."

Amirah scooped up all the stray banana peels and put them neatly on the tray.

"Come on Dad, what happened after that?"

"Well, like I said, I just stood there holding back a flood of tears, expecting them to charge at me and finish me off and before I knew it, Ted, that's his name, started backing off and gesturing to his friends to get out of there quick smart!"

"You're kidding. You never beat him up."

"Didn't have to. I scared the daylights out of him just letting him see what I could do and let his imagination do the rest. It is all from Allah. He protected me. Those guys were dangerous."

"But you said the kids used to call it your 'bonkers session', so they still teased you."

"Oh yes, they have to feel they have the upper hand, but they teased from a distance."

"Do you know what happened to them later, I mean, when they grew up?"

"Not all of them but I know that Ted, the mean fella', ended up in prison. Robbed a milk bar and because he had a handgun when he did it, he lost how many years of his life for a few hundred dollars."

"Wow," was all Amirah could say.

"Do you like to hear my old stories?"

"I love it, Dad. I wish you could have told me all this before."

"I didn't think you'd like it but then, I don't always remember things until the subject comes up."

"I am growing up Dad. I really want to *know* you and what you were like when you were little. Not just normal stuff but how you lived your life and grew up and all that because I'm finding it a bit hard."

Amirah looked puzzled.

"Are you? Sorry to hear that."

Adam went over next to Amirah and gave her a big hug.

"Growing up is not easy for anyone and I know that it must be hard not having your mum around."

There! He said it. He couldn't see Amirah's face because she was nestled into his shoulder. His dark blue eyes were squeezed shut and two tears found their way out of the corners of his eyes.

CHAPTER 4

Road Runner

Amirah rugged up against the cold and took an old blanket and her school bag filled with food and books. Together, she and her father headed off towards the beach. The air was chilled, but the sun shone warmly as they walked slowly along the sandy path that led from their small wooden house to the seashore. As they were walking, Amirah stopped and turned around, wishing to get a fuller picture of the 'Retreat' as they called it; a place where she had stayed off and on since she could remember.

The Retreat was a large rectangular box-shaped building with a sloping roof that collected rainwater into a tank at the side. A wooden veranda surrounded the front of the house, with thick posts spaced out across its edge. Five steps led down to the garden path that continued onto the sandy trail on which Amirah and her father were now strolling. The front windows were huge and enabled the people inside to see the beachfront from wherever they might sit. Soft green curtains hung on the sides of the windows from the inside and on the outside strong wooden shutters were fixed to the frames, ready to be closed to ward off severe storms and strong winds. The garden at the front was simply various sized trees and bushes with wildflowers growing wherever they chose. Birds flew freely from tree to tree without threat of harm or disturbance. The brown color of the house and the greenness that surrounded it made it appear to be almost absorbed into the surrounding bush land. The house lay on the side of a small hill that continued behind it. The walk to the beach was easy and the land sloped gently away to make room for the deep golden sand.

"What a beautiful sight," commented Amirah.

"What in particular?" asked her dad.

"Just everything around here," she responded, almost in a whisper. "Everything seems so peaceful, so natural. I feel happy here."

"Me too," he said, smiling. "Nature always calms me down," he observed. "That's why we used to come here a lot in the early days."

"You mean you and Mum?"

"Yes, and you, too."

"Who built this place?"

"Well, it was your mum's dowry when we got married. The land was a part of my inheritance from my father and your mum wanted to build a house on it so we could come here whenever we had the chance."

"So did Mum actually design it?"

"Yes. Being an architect made that easy for her. She always liked simple, uncomplicated things. This house is a reflection of her."

Birds chirped noisily overhead and some movement in the nearby bushes made Amirah turn her head to see a kangaroo bound quickly out of sight.

"Did you see that, Dad?" asked Amirah excitedly.

"You'll see more of those fellows around sunset. That's when they come out to feed. Your mum used to feed them by hand. They knew she wouldn't hurt them."

"Animals are clever, aren't they Dad?"

"Smarter than some people."

"How?" asked Amirah.

"They simply do what comes naturally to them. They don't take from this earth more than what they need, and they don't harm it."

Amirah smiled, "Yeah wombats don't throw their garbage out the window."

"Neither do kangaroos! By the way, are you going to swim today?" asked Adam. There was a challenging tone to his voice.

"No thanks. It's way too cold for me. Are you?" asked Amirah looking at her father uncertainly.

"I thought I might take a bit of a dip."

"It's freezing Dad. Maybe you'll get sick."

"*Inshaa Allah* I won't. You're getting soft Princess," smiled her dad. "I thought you said that I was the wimp!"

"*Was* Dad! Past tense! Not anymore. You've got that look on your face. I know you're going to chuck me in!"

Amirah laughed and backed off.

"It might cool down your temper a bit. Heard you've been punching girls at school," said Adam with a villainous expression.

He threw off his comfy trainers and pullover, leaving only a t-shirt and cut-off denim jeans.

"Now, would you like to go swimming with your jacket on or off?" asked Adam cheekily.

Amirah knew she'd better take her jacket off or else there would be nothing to warm herself in when she got out of the water.

She was still backing away from Adam, but she had dropped her bag and kicked off her trainers. There was no use escaping the fact that she was going for a swim that day whether she liked it or not.

"Now what's the use of having all your skills girl, when you're too soft to get into a little bit of water?"

As soon as he spoke a rather large wave spilled over and crashed against the shore.

"That's not a bit of water Dad. That's the ocean you know. The great depths of the sea. No one knows what's going on under there and we just step into it or get chucked into it as in my case," she laughed, almost breathless as she anticipated the cold. "And we don't even know what's hanging around down there searching for lunch!"

"Well, if a hungry shark comes along just put him in a headlock!" sneered her dad.

"I was thinking I'd call you to finish him off."

"Me and a shark! No way! You'll see me running off along those hills," said Adam, pointing to his right where rolling green hills edged their way up the slope towards their house.

"Oh well, if you can't beat 'em, join 'em," said Amirah as she jumped into the water.

"That's not fair," cried Adam. "Now I miss the pleasure of chucking you in!"

"That's one for me," said Amirah through chattering teeth. "It's freezing in here, Dad!"

"Keep moving and start swimming, you'll warm up."

Adam dived under the next wave and Amirah waited for him to bob up out of the water, but she couldn't see him. She waited and waited for what seemed like ages and then she started to feel afraid. Suddenly, she felt something pulling at her leg and thoughts of the shark that she had just been joking about came to mind. She screamed and jumped around frantically. Just at that moment, her father's curly head and smiling face bobbed out of the waves and she turned to him furiously.

"Dad! You scared the life out of me!" she squealed.

She started splashing him and to her annoyance, a wave caught her from behind and sent her reeling. It pushed her under the water, and she opened her eyes and saw the sandy seabed. The water was pushing her down. Two strong arms grabbed her and pulled her to the surface.

"You all right Princess?"

"Yes, I think so," spluttered Amirah. "Just a bit out of breath."

"Come on then, let's go and get warmed up. Enough for one day."

Adam pulled her onto his back and carried her onto shore.

"Thought I was too big for this," commented Amirah, feeling safe now.

"Not yet," he assured her.

Amirah scanned the horizon. There was no one around for miles; just her and her dad and the sea and the sky.

CHAPTER 5

Admissions

Amirah wrapped herself in her jacket, and Adam pulled a large beach towel out of his bag.

"Here, cover yourself in this," he said as he tossed it over her head.

While Amirah sat shivering on the dry sand, Adam ran to the nearby bushland and gathered a large bundle of wood, sticks and dry leaves. He returned, and in a few minutes, there was a small fire burning beside Amirah. The leaves crackled and the sticks burned easily. Amirah rubbed her hands over the warmth and smiled up to her dad.

"This is really great. We're so lucky to have this place and the chance to come here."

Her smile warmed his heart.

"Don't you ever get cold Dad?"

"Yeah, I get cold."

"You don't wear a lot of clothes?"

"I got used to dressing lightly, and I wear my jacket. After a while, you toughen up and feel comfortable."

"I can't do that."

"It's not necessary. Do what makes you feel comfortable." Adam opened his knap sack again and took out a bag of marshmallows.

"Toasted marshmallows! Great surprise Dad. It's not every day you eat junk food."

"True but this is a special occasion."

"I thought people were supposed to eat toasted marshmallows at night in front of an open fire."

"Now who made that rule?" laughed Adam, who always went to bed early.

Amirah was handed the first one. It was white and soft.

"Dad."

"Yes."

"You said before that this place is a reflection of Mum."

"That's right."

"What did you mean exactly?"

"Well, I meant that she made it exactly the way she wanted it. Right down to the cups and cushions, and little odds and ends. This place was just land and she built everything on it."

Adam stared towards the house and could see part of the roof between some tall trees.

"I guess you have a lot of memories here, Dad."

"I certainly do. Precious memories."

"Can you share them with me, Dad? You see, I hardly remember anything. I was very small when Mum, well, left us."

Adam looked at her. He felt scared inside; it was a feeling not unlike the one he had when he was a little boy hiding behind those shelter sheds. Amirah looked at him kindly, with gentle eyes.

"I see so much of your mum in you."

"Really? Granny said the same thing the other day."

"It's true."

"Does that bother you?"

"Why would it? I loved your Mum and I love you. Having you resemble her just makes me remember her and my memories of her are good."

Adam turned his attention towards the sea and didn't speak for a little while.

"Your Mum was a gentle and kind lady. She had confidence and dignity. I never once heard her raise her voice except one time when she dropped a pot on her foot."

Adam smiled in spite of himself. Amirah didn't interrupt him. She was scared that if she did, he might back off and stop talking. She had longed to hear him talk like this.

"I was playing with you in the living room. It was here at the Retreat, and I honestly nearly had a heart attack. She had broken two toes. She was in a lot of pain, and I drove her to the hospital in town straight away."

"How old was I then?"

"About one and a half. I was teaching you to kick in those days."

"Wow, I can't remember that," marveled Amirah. She wished she could remember every detail.

"You know Dad, all I remember of Mum is the shape of her eyes and I remember feeling nice and safe and warm."

Tears sprung to her eyes. She had told herself that she would be brave.

"I guess I'm the wimp now," said Amirah, trying to smile.

"You're no wimp Princess."

They sat in silence for a few minutes.

"Dad, why don't you like to talk about Mum since all your memories of her are good?" asked Amirah, venturing to ask a question, any question that would give her all the information she needed.

"It's because my memories of her are good that I feel this pain," said Adam, pointing to his chest.

He couldn't look at Amirah now and his gaze scanned the horizon that lay misleadingly close, beyond the waves.

"See, when we came to know that your mum was sick, you were a bit more than two years old."

"You mean you didn't know she was sick all along?"

"No. Cancer just kind of sneaks up on you sometimes and she seemed healthy but then started to feel really tired and got a pain in her side that wouldn't go away. She went to all kinds of doctors and in the end, they told her she'd had this for some time and that now things had gone too far, and it was just well, a matter of time."

"How long did she have when you got to know all this?" Amirah spoke quietly, almost a whisper.

"They told us, only Allah knows of course, about a year."

Amirah scratched the crisp golden sand with her toe and started to dig a little hole. A cloud moved in front of the sun and for a minute or so, the sky darkened. Everything to do with this subject was associated with pain and now she felt it so deeply that she wondered how her dad had managed to keep a cheery face most of the time. Mustn't be such a wimp after all. She looked at him lovingly and gave him a reassuring smile.

"Are you ready for more Princess?" asked her father gently.

"Yes Dad, if you are," answered Amirah softly.

"I freaked out and got all emotional and angry, but she had far more self-control and faith than I did. She just turned to the Qur'an and started to pray more than ever. I used to see her in *Sujood,* and she would stay there for a long, long time. After a while, she made her peace with Allah, and accepted her fate. I can't express to you the peace she had on her face all throughout that year and three months."

"Did you do the same Dad? Did you pray more and all that?"

"Of course. When any calamity strikes what else can we do but turn to Allah? I know that now and I knew that then, but her faith must have run deeper than mine because I just couldn't find the same peace that she found." Adam looked troubled.

"Was Mum in hospital?"

"Not until the very end. She stayed a lot of the time here and when I had to go to work, good old Granny would come and stay with her. They used to get along so well *Mashaa Allah*." Adam smiled.

"Did Granny get all emotional?"

"Yes, at times she would break down, but she has a lot of faith and as she's got older, she seems permanently at peace. May Allah bless her. She's helped me so much in my life."

"Me too," added Amirah with a sigh. "I get the picture. I know it's hard for you to talk about all this."

"It's not finished. I'm going to tell you everything," said Adam, turning to face her. He was huddled in his huge beach towel and his feet were tucked under him with his hands resting comfortably on his lap.

"I'm going to stop running away from this, *Inshaa Allah*," he said with an air of determination that made Amirah stop and looked at him intently.

"Your Mum never asked me for anything really, throughout the whole ordeal. She plodded on, trusting in Allah but there was one thing she asked me to do, and I promised."

"What was that?" asked Amirah.

"She didn't want to die alone. She told me that she knew I couldn't do anything for her, but she just wanted me to be there. You see, she always thought I was very strong."

Adam was sad and disappointed in himself. He started digging in the sand with his hands as he talked.

"Can we walk a bit, Dad? I don't feel so cold now."

She sensed his unease and wanted to help him, and she knew he liked to move around when he was upset.

"That sounds good, I feel like moving a bit."

Adam jumped to his feet.

Amirah smiled, "Dad. You're not going to run, are you?"

"No, I won't," he reassured her.

They left their things where they were. The fire had nearly burned itself out and all that was left were a few shining red twigs. They headed off down the sandy coast. Amirah reached out and took his hand and he squeezed it gently, tugging her along. After a few minutes they started to talk again.

"Well," he continued, "I kept vigil over her, especially after she went to the hospital and only left her to work or take my turn with you."

"Where was I?"

"At Granny's place, and Granny and I took turns staying with you but then one day you got a fever and Granny had to stay with you when it was her turn to stay with your Mum, so I went to the hospital that day. Problem was that I had a competition that night, a big one and your Mum insisted that I go. If I won, the prize money would help pay some of the bills which were piling up. Anyway, in the end I let her convince me to go and after I finished my piece, I rushed back and ... Oh Allah ... she was gone by the time I returned."

Adam kind of moaned these last words. They came from a place deep inside him; a place that was still disturbed after many years.

Tears poured down Amirah's cheeks, but she made no sound. She wasn't sure who she was crying for, her Mum, her dad or for herself. Adam held onto the small hand and stopped. He too was holding back tears.

"See, all this time I felt guilty! I broke my promise to the person who shared my life and had done so much for me and put up with so much from me."

Adam was almost shouting now.

"How could I be so selfish?" he called out. He closed his eyes and felt the wind and the sea spray on his face. He breathed in deeply and hung his head.

Amirah let go of his hand and wiped her face. It frightened her to see her dad like that.

She pulled at his arm and led him over to a grassy slope and tugged at him to sit down beside her. He sat quietly and said no more.

"Why don't you go for a bit of a run, Dad?"

"I feel tired."

She patted his back. She was scrambling for words. "Don't worry. I'm sure she forgave you. After all, she told you to go."

"That's what Granny always says," he responded.

"We all make mistakes Dad and you never meant not to be there," Amirah said anxiously.

"I've thought of all these things, but they never seem to help," he said sadly.

Amirah thought for some time. She turned towards the sea and noticed its brilliant color of azure blue that seemed to melt into the sky. She felt a longing to belong - to blend with nature that always brought peace to her heart despite its strength and sometimes harshness.

Some moments passed.

"You always told me, Dad, that we belong to Allah before we belong to anyone else, right?"

"Right, Princess."

"Well, Mum belongs to Allah and maybe He wanted her to be only with Him at that moment."

Adam looked up and his eyes caught her gaze.

"Maybe you're upsetting yourself over something that Allah wanted and maybe it was good for Mum. After all, you told me she prayed so much and was close to Allah, so surely everything was for her good." Amirah patted his hand gently.

Amirah wanted him to feel at peace. If she had it and could give it to him, she would.

"That's a really good way of looking at things. *Jazaka Allahu khairan.*" Adam looked at Amirah intently. "She really is growing up," he thought.

"*Wa iyyak,* Dad."

They both sat in silence for a long time, each one busy with their own thoughts. The sun had begun its decline and the night would soon arrive. They started back to the house and collected their things on the way. Hardly a word was spoken. There was no need to talk really. Everything had already been said and now Amirah had begun to understand her dad in a way that she had never done before. The closeness she felt with him filled the void that had haunted her for years. Surely Allah brings relief.

CHAPTER 6

Choices

Later that night, when Amirah was tucked in and ready to sleep, her father came and sat down on her bed. He smiled. Since they came home, they had both been busy with their own things. Adam cooked the chops and made a delicious dinner and Amirah had read her books and written some things in her diary.

Dinner had been somewhat quiet and peaceful.

"Something else I have to talk to you about Princess," said Adam with his usual smile and calm.

"What's that?"

"Well, I've been offered a job. It's something I've wanted for a long time, and I think it's a great opportunity for me and for us."

Adam paused, waiting for it all to sink in. Amirah was wondering what on earth it could be about. Surely it must have something to do with his writing.

"What kind of job Dad? Is it your writing or your karate?" asked Amirah, feeling rather curious.

"Something to do with my writing," he answered.

"I just knew it!" responded Amirah.

"Actually, a magazine has offered me a year's contract to work in a foreign country."

"Which country?" asked Amirah, sitting up in bed. Her eyes were wide open, and she felt excited.

"Guess," said Adam with a cheeky smile.

"Give me some hints then," answered Amirah, her eyes shining.

"It's north of here," said Adam, his eyes twinkling.

"Well Dad, that includes most of the world. We're

in the bottom of Australia!"

"Somewhere in Africa."

"In the jungle!"

"No, further up. Real old place with lots of history."

"Sorry Dad, but the world was created at the same time so how can one place be older than the rest?"

"Don't be smart, you know what I mean!" said Adam. "Quit stalling and guess."

"How far up north?"

"Right up there!"

"On the Mediterranean Sea?"

"You got it."

"Wow. Let me think. Must be - maybe - Libya!"

"Nope, next door neighbor."

"Then...hmmm... Egypt!" cried out Amirah eagerly.

"Yep! You got it."

"For a whole year. That's great. Which part?"

"The capital city. Do you know its name?"

"Cairo!"

"That's the place."

"Where will we stay?"

"Well, that's what I want you to think about Princess," he said seriously.

"I can take you, but I want you to think carefully."

"You want me to go?" asked Amirah, feeling suddenly worried.

"Yes, I always want you to be near me, but you have to keep some things in mind."

"Like what?" Amirah could feel her face growing red.

"Granny will be here and then there's your school and your friends."

"That's a bit of a joke. I don't really have many friends."

"Well, it will be a new place and your Arabic is Okay, but the people speak in a dialect, not classical Arabic."

"You mean they won't understand me if I talk?"

"Educated people will understand you but they're not used to people speaking like that, so it will sound a bit strange to them. Anyway, I'm sure you'll pick it up, but you should think about it carefully and, remember, if you decide you'd like to stay back here with Granny, I won't be upset."

Amirah felt troubled. She would have preferred him to be upset. She had a rather odd feeling inside. She would have preferred that he insisted she go. She wondered if he wanted to get rid of her. It was an awful thought. Adam saw a disturbed look on her face and thought she must be thinking about what to do.

"Don't answer me now Princess. Think about it and we'll talk on the weekend, *Inshaa Allah*."

He kissed her good night and left.

Amirah lay in bed for a long time. This was Tuesday and there were still three days to go until the weekend. What a day it had been! Just when she thought they had come to terms about the story of her mum, he had to go and throw this at her. Deep inside she started to feel rather angry. It was a feeling that could rise and nearly choke her.

Thoughts flooded her mind. Was he trying to palm her off? Did he want a year of freedom? She shuddered. Feeling very restless, she got out of bed quietly and went to the bathroom and made *wudu'*. She put on her long prayer dress and faced the *Qibla* and started to pray two *rak`ahs*. The day's emotion caught up with her. As she read the Qur'an, tears welled in her eyes, as she poured her heart out to Allah, the only One who can help.

From the other room, Adam heard her movements and came through to check on her. He peeped inside her room and found her absorbed in prayer. He smiled with satisfaction and felt at peace. He knew it was a big decision for her to make but he thought it was important that she had a choice in the matter. She was getting too big to be ordered around and if a choice was available, he wanted to give it to her. He hoped she would want to go with him, but he was determined to respect her decision. He quietly left her room and went to bed.

CHAPTER 7

Mrs. Jones

Amirah returned to school with a lot on her mind. She felt a lot closer to her dad but the decision she had to make weighed heavily on her. Thoughts troubled her.

"Does Dad want me to go with him? Am I just in his way?" she thought.

She felt confused and on edge. She had just a few days to make a big decision and she didn't know what to do. She approached her school building and paused, looking at the chattering children hurrying along. A few of the kids waved and she waved back. She wondered what the day would hold but her heart wasn't really in it. She sighed when she saw her teacher, but then heard the first bell and quickened her pace.

※

Mrs. Jones, the school principal, was not new at Amirah's school. She was as old and solid as the building itself. She was part of the very foundation of this institution of learning, and it was a part of her. She commanded respect from everyone she dealt with. Although she never raised her voice, except to a rather high-pitched tone, people listened to her and rarely argued. She was organized, committed and a perfectionist. She belonged to the 'old school' and found it somewhat difficult to adopt the new teaching methods that had been introduced. This was her final year of teaching, for the following year she would retire - not from choice, but the law admitted no compromise, something Mrs. Jones understood completely, and she submitted from her heart.

Amirah was known as an intelligent girl and was admired and befriended by some and envied by many. Although they tagged her with names like 'snowball', she didn't yet realize that their viciousness was motivated by the desire to topple her, for indeed, she was attractive, kind, and clever - a combination that few can attain. However, everyone has their weak point and Amirah's was mathematics. She felt more at home in the subjects based on language and expression, so mathematics came as a bit of a chore. It so happened that Mrs. Jones was to herald in her final year of teaching by taking on the role of math's teacher for Amirah's class.

Amirah was no stranger to Mrs. Jones. She'd had the pleasure of awarding the young girl certificates and prizes for excellent results, good behavior, and the student most likely to succeed. The fact that Amirah was one of the few Muslims who attended her school, didn't bother Mrs. Jones as much as the fact that she was the only girl who insisted on dressing modestly, and even took permission from the board of education to accommodate the school uniform to suit her needs. This was something unthinkable to Mrs. Jones, who after refusing to give permission to Adam, had received a call from the board of education telling her to allow Amirah to alter the uniform, if the colour and style remained the same. It had become something of a cold war between them. Something Amirah found difficult to understand.

Amirah ran quickly to catch up with her class who were walking single file into the school building. She reached the end of the line as they rounded the corner to her classroom, to be met by Mrs. Jones at the door. Mrs. Jones eyed Amirah as she put her books neatly into her locker and her school bag under it. The young girl wore navy pants under her navy-blue dress, which had been lengthened slightly. Her white blouse and navy-blue jumper were spotless, and her white cotton scarf was pinned tidily and gave a graceful look to the tall, slender figure. Her white socks and shiny black shoes were as they should be. In fact, Mrs. Jones had nothing to complain about. Amirah walked past her new teacher and said, 'Good morning Mrs. Jones."

Mrs. Jones grunted something in reply and told everyone to sit down. They did.

※

In many classrooms there is a troublemaker; a ringleader who brings behind them a following of people with weak character and a desire to be better than all the others. In Amirah's class it was Tina Taylor. Amirah didn't know too much about Tina except that she had a wicked tongue and a sarcastic manner that had thrown Amirah into many upsetting situations.

Tina waged war against quite a few members of her class and had a special derogatory name for each of her victims. Gina, the Italian girl didn't know how to speak English as well as everyone else; Debbie was very tall for her age and had the habit of bending over slightly at the shoulders to appear shorter; Judith ate too much and was overweight, and Amirah was different. As well as being 'different', Amirah was also not easily ruffled like the others. Tina saw it as a contest, and she took up the challenge with a fighting spirit. She had only managed to make Amirah angry once and the result of that was a stinging punch from the usually quiet, refined girl. That punch had cost Tina a lot in the eyes of her friends and by the time Amirah had returned to school after the long weekend, Tina was ready for her. It was more of a need than a desire, for so much of her self-esteem depended on the opinion of her friends.

※

Being the last to enter the room, it was easy to notice Amirah, who quietly arranged her books on the table she shared with Stacey Dennison. The perimeter of the classroom was lined with tables, which left an empty space in the center of the room. The teacher's desk was just a little to the left of the whiteboard and Mrs. Jones filled it with her daunting figure.

"Good morning girls," said Mrs. Jones with a cool expression.

"Good morning, Mrs. Jones," was the apathetic reply.

"I have some news for you all. As you know this is my final year of teaching after which I shall retire."

A few sniggers emerged from the crowd of girls, but it was impossible to tell the guilty parties.

"Quiet please! So, I want to make it clear that in all my many years of teaching none of my students have ever failed. Do you all understand that?"

"Yes Mrs. Jones."

"Do you understand what I mean, Amirah Stevenson?"

Amirah was a bit shocked that she had been singled out. She nodded her head in reply.

Mrs. Jones looked at her seriously.

"I don't want any students to fail mathematics this year," she repeated.

All the girls had turned towards Amirah, thinking that since Mrs. Jones had mentioned her especially, it was better to concentrate on her rather than on any of the others that her point could have just as well been directed to. Tina was sitting opposite Amirah and sat back smugly with her arms folded across her chest in a defiant, proud manner.

"I understand, Mrs. Jones," replied Amirah, her cheeks flaming red.

"Good. So, I have decided that every week we will have a quiz and the results of that quiz will combine towards the final grade. I am taking all these quizzes and so forth very seriously and I expect you will all do the same. Failure to do so will not be pleasant, let me assure you."

Mrs. Jones surveyed the faces that stared at her with a mixture of surprise and disbelief.

"We will begin today. I will go to my office now and get the quiz papers and in the meantime, you will kindly rearrange your seats. Mrs. Jones then told each girl where she was to sit, then she left the room.

Amirah stared in horror. Mrs. Jones had instructed her to sit next to Tina during the quiz. Equally surprised, Tina nodded to her friend Nicole and beckoned her to come over.

"Don't worry Nikky. I'll quickly write down some of the important things on a paper and hand it to you while *old stone* face isn't looking."

"How can you do that when she said 'snowball' will sit between us?"

"Let me take care of that," said Tina defiantly.

Amirah convinced herself not to get upset. After all, she only had to sit next to Tina for the quiz then she would be able to go back to her own table. Resigned, Amirah took a pen and went to sit between Tina and Nicole. The rest of the class watched rather intently as Amirah sat down between her enemies; girls she would much rather have befriended.

"Hey Snowball," said Tina.

"I have a name and you can use it if you want to talk to me," said Amirah indignantly.

"I don't have to call you nothing," whispered Tina, "you just listen to me and do as you're told."

"Since when do I have to listen to you?"

"Since now."

Without waiting for a reply Tina added, "After a little while I'm going to pass a paper to you under the desk and you're going to slip it to Nicole."

"Are you going to cheat?" asked Amirah.

The whole class started to laugh. After all, what did it matter, they thought if they passed the test.

"What's your problem? It will be a miracle if you pass," sneered Tina.

"I'd rather fail than cheat and I won't help you do it," said Amirah with such determination that a hush fell over the rest of the class as they sat wondering what would happen next.

CHAPTER 8

Caught Red Handed!

Before the girls could continue their conversation, Mrs. Jones entered the classroom once more.

"I don't need to tell you girls that this is to be treated like a formal exam and there is to be no talking and so on. Is that clear?"

"Yes, Mrs. Jones," came the resounding answer.

All eyes were on Amirah, who sat staring at the desk in front of her. She felt butterflies in her stomach, and it reminded her of her father's story about the bully who beat him at school. She didn't dare turn towards Tina or Nicole, so she simply looked ahead of her and waited for her test paper to be placed in front of her.

Soon the whole class was concentrating on their quiz papers and Amirah was lost in algebra and forgot all about Tina.

"Psst," whispered a voice next to her.

Amirah turned her head and saw Tina watching Mrs. Jones who was searching for something in the cupboard. She had seen her chance to pass the paper to Nicole through Amirah.

Amirah looked at Tina and then at the paper and simply shook her head and continued with her work.

Tina was a rather short girl with long, straight, shiny, black hair. Her eyes were deep green with specks of brown and she had a few sandy freckles on her face. Her short nose was accentuated by the broadness of her mouth and jaw. She sat glaring at Amirah's calm appearance. She felt angry, and the bitterness of her thoughts disfigured the contours of her face. She could not bear to think that Amirah had won their battle. Again. No, that was just too much!

She wasn't quite sure why she disliked Amirah. After all, everyone knew that Amirah didn't have a mother and that her father was weird, and she dressed differently. She was good at school except for mathematics, and she kept to herself. Nevertheless, she just didn't like her. Without much fore-thought Tina took the small scrap of paper and threw it onto Amirah's lap, then she shouted out, "Mrs. Jones! Amirah Stevenson is cheating!"

Amirah froze.

"What's this?" cried Mrs. Jones. "Is there a girl in my class who is cheating?" Mrs. Jones stomped over to the table where Amirah and Tina were sitting, and sure enough on Amirah's lap lay a small piece of scrap paper. Mrs. Jones scooped it up and scrutinized it.

"Amirah Stevenson! Stand up!"

"Mrs. Jones, please!" cried Amirah, looking at Tina and then at Nicole. Tears poured down her cheeks and she had the feeling to run.

"Be quiet! Go and stand in the corner over there

this instant!"

It was the first time in many years of teaching that Mrs. Jones had shouted. Everyone sat in silence and alarm. Tina sat in her place with a big smirk on her face and winked at Nicole who stared blankly at Amirah. All the girls were glad they were not Amirah Stevenson that day.

Mrs. Jones walked straight up to where Amirah was standing and put her face close to hers and said in a raspy voice, "I thought Muslims were supposed to be honest!"

The words struck Amirah in the heart. How much worse could things get?

She had to stay in the corner until recess. She attended the other classes, but everything seemed to be happening in a whirl. She didn't really hear what the teachers were saying. It was all a blur. Everyone came to know what had happened and the girls whispered and sniggered at her. Amirah tried so hard not to cry but from time to time the injustice of the situation dawned on her and she couldn't help it. Mrs. Jones had told everyone in the class that a decision about Amirah's 'situation' would be made before the end of the day. Most of the girls thought she would be suspended and have a black mark next to her name. No one listened to her, and no one dared to go against Tina and Nicole, and *they* would never tell the truth.

Mrs. Jones entered the classroom during the geography lesson and spoke without even excusing herself to the teacher.

"Amirah Stevenson! Your grandmother has been called to the school and you are to meet me in my office in five minutes."

Amirah's heart sank. She did not want her Granny to see her in such a humiliating situation. After five minutes, she was outside Mrs. Jones' office and sure enough down the corridor walked her Granny. She appeared quite tall as she glided along the polished floor.

"*As salam alaikum* Princess," she said cheerily.

"*Wa alaikum assalam* Granny," replied Amirah, feeling a bit puzzled. "Granny doesn't look angry," she thought to herself.

"What's up?" asked Granny, seating herself next to Amirah.

Amirah explained what had happened and Granny listened. Then she saw the flicker of a smile on her face.

When she finished her story, Amirah couldn't help

but ask, "Granny, why are you smiling?"

"Well, today's an important day, dear."

"Important isn't the word I would have chosen," commented Amirah, feeling depressed.

"It's not as it seems. The world is full of injustice and foolishness, and this is just another example. I'm sure it's not the first or the last time such things have happened, but I think Mrs. Jones is in for a bit of a surprise."

"Mrs. Jones! Surprise? I don't understand Granny."

"You see, Mrs. Jones and I go back a long way."

Amirah looked incredulously at Granny.

"How?"

"She and I used to go to school together. I have lived in this part of the city most of my life and I know a lot of people. I could tell you some stories about Mrs. Jones!"

"Granny!"

"Don't worry dear. This will all be sorted before you know it."

"So, you believe me?"

"Don't be ridiculous. Of course, I do. I know my girl and I know there is some kind of misunderstanding. I don't know what happened, but I do know you are no cheat."

Amirah felt as if a weight had been lifted from her heart. She felt that it wasn't important what the rest of them thought if Granny trusted her. After a minute or so Mrs. Jones appeared at the doorway of her office.

"I believe you are the grandmother of Amirah Stevenson," stated Mrs. Jones arrogantly and without any kind of polite introduction.

"Good morning Mrs. Jones, I hope you are well and yes, I am this girl's grandmother and I'd like to have a word with you if you don't mind."

Granny didn't wait for a reply but simply got off her chair, marched past the startled head mistress and sat down in her office in front of the huge mahogany desk.

"Well, I never," started Mrs. Jones, trying to compose herself. "Come inside Amirah, come inside."

"Oh no," said Granny. "Amirah will sit where she is until I've finished and if you don't mind, I'd like to get started. I have many important things to do today."

Mrs. Jones didn't know how to react. She looked at Amirah who tried to appear inconspicuous and then at Granny sitting on the leather chair with a beaming, confident smile, and she went into the office and banged the door behind her.

CHAPTER 9

Camelia Dirtmouthe

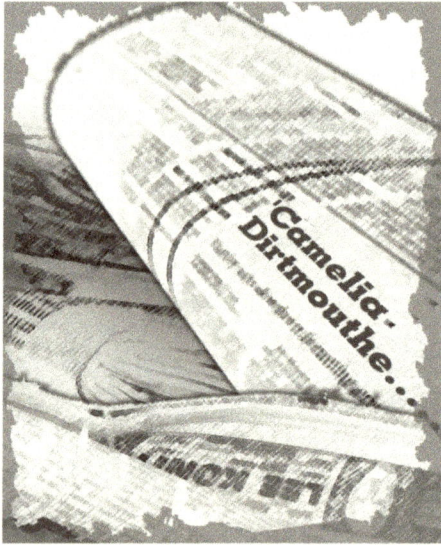

A short time later, Granny emerged from the office, her head held high and a smile on her face.

"I'll take my girl home now, Mrs. Jones but she will be at school tomorrow *Inshaa Allah*. She has been through quite an ordeal today and I don't wish her to go through anymore. I trust that you understand what I said and that all this will be properly sorted out by tomorrow."

Granny didn't wait for a response but spoke to Amirah quietly.

"Where is your bag dear?"

"Down the hall."

"Okay. Let's go and get it. It's time to go home."

Granny walked with Amirah to her locker and took her books and her bag. They walked out of the school building and over to the car park.

Once they were home, Granny made Amirah freshen up while she prepared some food and a nice hot cup of herbal tea.

"There now dear. Drink this and eat up, you'll soon feel better again *Inshaa Allah*."

Amirah still felt quite shaken.

"Granny, does Dad know?"

"Yes. I called him and told him."

Amirah felt worried.

"Was he mad?"

"Why should he be?"

"I was accused of cheating."

"Accused is one thing, proof is another."

"I had the paper on my lap."

"Once the accused pleads 'not guilty', there must be an investigation, right?"

"Right."

"Was there an investigation dear?"

"No, there wasn't."

Amirah felt sad.

"Granny, I don't have any friends. No one stood up for me. They all knew what Tina was going to do, and no one said a word."

"Hmm …. But I suppose they were afraid of Tina and of course, of Mrs. Jones as well."

"That doesn't help my problem Granny. Now the school thinks I'm a cheat."

"Did you pray and ask Allah to make things clear?"

"I made a lot of *du`aa* Granny."

"Then be patient and you'll see things will be set aright."

"You sound confident Granny. Is there something else going on?"

"You know Amirah, Allah gave us a brain to think and do our best, and at the same time we trust Him.

That's how things work. When I got that phone call today, I must say I was a bit shocked and upset, so I made *du`aa* and asked Allah for help and guidance. I know without any doubt Princess, that Allah answers our *du`aa*. Then I got to thinking about things and I remembered something and felt better."

"What was that?"

Granny sat quietly, thinking. She and Amirah were sitting in the living room on the sofa and Granny was stretched out and reclining comfortably in her chair.

"By the way Granny, before you tell me, I have to tell you something."

"What's that?"

"When I was staying at the Retreat with Dad, he told me some things about you, and I was surprised."

"Yes, he told me."

"You never told me about your self-defense and all that."

"It's not that important dear."

"I think it is," commented Amirah. "And well, when I saw you marching down the corridor today, the thought crossed my mind that maybe you might have a go at Mrs. Jones."

Granny laughed out loud.

"Oh! You are funny sometimes Amirah. There's no need to get physical every time you have a problem!"

"But I get all worked up and worried and anxious and then I start to feel angry."

"But dear, you don't fight with someone who can't defend themselves and Mrs. Jones' bark is a lot worse than her bite."

"Her bite was hard today, Granny. She is mean."

"It's easy to do things like that to kids but with me, believe me, she was a mouse when I had her alone in the office."

"Really?"

"Yes dear."

"This is all very strange," commented Amirah.

"It is," asserted Granny.

"Another thing Granny. Dad told me you didn't help him when he was at school and facing bullies."

"Oh Amirah! I helped him… in other ways. I wanted him to stand up for himself and realize he could protect himself."

Amirah thought about this. "But Granny, you came to the school and helped me. What's different?"

Granny held Amirah's hand and said softly, "You, my dear, were not facing kids who are bullies. You were facing a figure of authority and you were not able to defend yourself. In this kind of situation an adult must step in."

"I see." Amirah was deep in thought.

After a few moments, Amirah asked, "What did you remember today?"

"Oh yes, well I remembered how this is her final year of teaching and how much she wants to go down in a blaze of glory, so to speak, and have everyone think highly of her. Then I remembered years ago when we were girls at school, she and I never really liked each other. She was always good at mathematics, but history was something else. Now I was good at history and a very similar situation happened to me like what happened to you today. But she was the one who accused me of cheating when it was really her."

"Really Granny?" asked Amirah, sitting forward in her chair.

"Yes, except that it was Camelia Dirtmouthe who set me up all those years ago."

"Who is Camelia Dirtmouthe?" asked Amirah,

confused.

"That was Mrs. Jones' name before she got married. Now it's Camelia Jones."

Amirah's eyes widened in surprise.

"So, I had the pleasure of reminding her of this little incident and inspired her to investigate the matter further and clear your name or else I would have my son write an article about it in the local newspaper."

"Granny! You didn't!"

"Yes, I did, and she backed right down and said how sure she was that there must have been some kind of misunderstanding because Amirah has always been a model student, bla, bla, bla."

"Granny, that's absolutely incredible."

"It's true and she knows it and I'm sure she doesn't want anyone else to know about it."

"But is it wrong to do that?"

"It is all true. I didn't make anything up. I call it 'motivation'."

There was no arguing with that.

"I'm sure, that *Inshaa Allah* when you go to school in the morning dear old Mrs. Dirtmouthe, I mean Jones, will have come up with something."

Amirah hoped Mrs. Jones would come up with a solution but she couldn't possibly imagine how the situation could be fixed!

CHAPTER 10

Tables Turned

The next afternoon Granny was sitting at her kitchen table as usual when she heard running footsteps up the garden path. She listened and then smiled and sat back waiting for the door to open.

A voice called out, "*As salam alaikum* Granny, it's me Amirah!"

"*Wa alaikum assalam.* Yes dear, come on in. I've

been waiting for you." Amirah was panting and poured herself some orange juice before she sat down at the kitchen table.

"Well, come on! I can't wait to know what happened today."

"You'll never guess Granny."

"Don't keep me in suspense. I'm getting older every minute dear," Granny smiled, and Amirah beamed back.

"Well, I went into class this morning and tried to keep myself inconspicuous, but it was hard. Everyone was whispering and staring at me, saying that I'd probably be suspended from school, and it was a black mark on my record and all that. Anyway, I didn't get into any arguments like you always say."

"Good dear, and then?"

"I had butterflies in my stomach and felt like I would throw up but then Mrs. Jones came in and she looked very stern. I can tell you my heart sank. Then I remembered your story about her yesterday, and Granny, I started to smile. I couldn't help it. I remembered you said her name was 'Dirtmouthe'. Oh, Granny! I couldn't help smiling. I wanted to laugh. I must have been nervous, and I couldn't control it, so I covered my mouth with my hand and put my head down. Tina was staring at me from across the room and she was a real smarty pants. Anyway, Mrs. Jones started to talk."

"What did good old Camelia have to say?"

"First, she called the class to attention and started to talk about how wrong it is to cheat and how people have lost their morals in this day and age and are prepared to do anything to succeed. I felt so embarrassed because everyone thought I was like that. I kept making *du`aa* and tried not to look at them. Then Mrs. Jones started to walk around the room, and she kept on talking. She started to raise her voice to a real high pitch, I had to stop myself from covering my ears. Anyway, she said that after what had happened yesterday, she felt very upset and could hardly believe that one of her pupils could stoop to such a cheap thing as cheating but then she added that there was something even worse than cheating and that was false accusation of a crime."

"Go on dear," said Granny, taking a big sip of her strawberry tea.

"She said that when she got home last night, she started thinking about me and how I was usually such a good student. So, she decided to double check the matter because she couldn't believe that I'd do something like that. Granny! She had taken out all the class workbooks and went through each one until she found the handwriting that most resembled that of the note I had been passed in class."

"Oh, poor soul, she stayed up all night. Good for her!" said Granny, "and then?"

"Well, she scared the life out of all of us and spun around and pointed with her finger at Tina Taylor and shouted - real loud Granny - for her to stand up. Well, Tina's face was white and all the girls were afraid. I can't begin to tell what Mrs. Jones said to her and Tina was so embarrassed that she started to cry and everyone, let me tell you Granny, *everyone* started to laugh at her. Even her friend Nicole laughed at her and teased her along with everyone else. It was so strange Granny. All her friends turned their backs on her."

"People are certainly very strange sometimes. It is indeed rare and difficult to find a true friend," noted Granny.

"I can see that. I was sure all the class liked her. She used to be the most popular girl in the class but now no one speaks to her, no one wants to sit next to her, and you know what else?"

"What dear?"

"They are all talking to me!"

"That is truly amazing."

"And to top it all off, Mrs. Jones made me stand up and gave me a public apology saying that she is deeply sorry for embarrassing me before she had investigated the matter thoroughly."

"And what did you say?"

"I just mumbled something. Can't even remember Granny. I was in shock!"

"Well, did you thank Allah dear?"

"Over and over again Granny. It is really a miracle how things turned around from being so absolutely terrible yesterday, to wonderfully good today!"

"It makes us remember never to give up hope. One never knows what lies just around the corner. And I'm so proud of you that you didn't lose your head and start saying silly things that you'd be sorry for now had you said them."

"True Granny."

Amirah jumped up and started giving Granny big hugs and kisses.

"I'm so glad I've got you Granny."

"And me too," replied Granny, returning the hug. "By the way dear, have you decided whether or not you're going to Egypt?"

Amirah pulled her face and said, "No Granny, I'll just stay with you, here at home."

Granny peered at the young girl from over the top of her spectacles and didn't speak for a moment.

"Where is your home dear?"

"Here with you Granny."

"Since when?"

"That's a funny question. Why do you ask?"

"Because this isn't your home dear."

Amirah felt afraid and didn't know what to say.

"What do you mean Granny? This is my home. I have a home with Dad and a home here."

"Wrong dear."

Amirah was puzzled.

"Can you explain what you mean Granny?" asked Amirah. She felt confused.

"Your home is with your father, wherever that may be. It may be in The Retreat, in a small house in town, here or in a tent in the desert. But wherever your dad is, that is your home. You and he belong together. I am your grandmother, and you can both come and stay here anytime. We are family and families stick together, but home, that is something else. It is a big word and doesn't so much refer to a place but to the people we are with."

Amirah was still confused, trying to understand what Granny meant.

"Can you say that in real English Granny?"

"Simply dear, you and your dad belong together. Your home is wherever he is, and you must be flexible enough to give up some things to be with him. I don't think you'd be happy without him."

Amirah knew that was true.

"But Granny, he will be busy in Egypt, and I'll just get in the way."

"What kind of nonsensical nonsense is that?" said Granny, looking quite wild. "Who said such a thing?"

"No one. Just me thinking."

"No that's not you dear, that's the *shaitan* and you're being foolish enough to listen. Well, just listen to me young lady, you belong with your dad, and that's that!"

"I know that Granny but honestly, does he want that?"

"You mean you're not sure if he wants you to go with him?" Granny couldn't believe what she was hearing.

"The thought had crossed my mind."

"Well, I never!" exclaimed Granny. "Just last night he sat in that chair and said he thinks you don't want to go with him because you'll miss me too much!"

"Did he?"

"And now you're sitting in the same place saying that you think he doesn't want you to go with him! I think it's time you both sat down and had a heart-to-heart talk. Again! Seems to be a communication breakdown somewhere along the line."

"Did he really say that Granny? So, he does want me to go with him?"

"Of course! He just wanted to give you the choice, so that you wouldn't feel obliged to go. He wants you to go with your heart at ease."

Amirah felt a wave of happiness come over her. All that silly worry had been for nothing.

CHAPTER 11

Time to Go

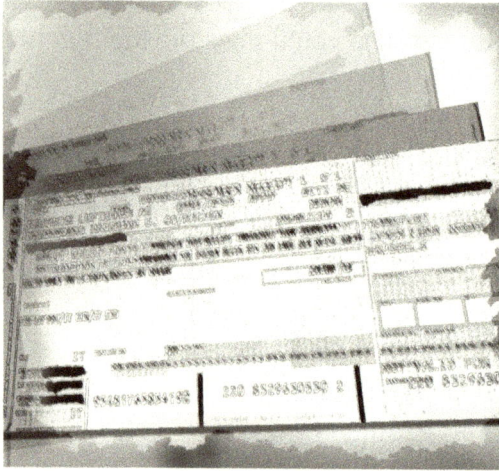

Adam came home a bit late that night and Amirah was waiting for him. It took a lot of effort not to close her eyes, but she was glad when the lock in the front door clicked, and the door opened.

"*As salam alaikum* Dad. I'm still awake."

"*Wa alaikum assalam*," he answered, slipping off his comfy trainers and putting away his briefcase and coat. "I'll be right with you, Princess."

Adam got himself a tray of fruit with bananas, apples, mandarins, grapes, and a handful of nuts.

"Having a snack before dinner, hey Dad?"

"Yeah, this is entrée. I've got bean sprouts, soaked chickpeas and a lettuce for main course!"

They both laughed together, and Amirah helped herself to an apple.

"So, Princess what have you decided about Egypt?"

"Well, Dad I prayed *Istikharah* and thought a lot and decided I have to be at home."

Adam had his mouth full of grapes and he stopped chewing for a second. His blue eyes were sad as he looked at her. He put his head down, trying not to show his disappointment.

After a bit he looked at her again, more composed, and said, "That's good. Whatever you want is what I want. I just want you to be happy and settled."

"Yeah, so what's the weather like in Egypt right now? Should I take my raincoat?" chuckled Amirah.

She had set him up and he fell for it. Adam was clearly surprised.

"I don't get it Princess. Why are you talking about your raincoat in Egypt?"

"Because I don't want to get wet!" Amirah laughed again.

Adam started to smile.

"What's going on?"

"I must be at home. I'm a kid, right? And well, Dad, you are my home. Where you go, I go! We're a package deal, so you'll just have to tell your magazine company that I must come too."

"I already did."

"What? How come? I only told you just now that I'm going!"

"I know but when it really came down to it, I thought to myself that if you decide not to go, I wouldn't know what to do without you, so I'd have to pull rank and order you to come. Tried to be democratic but naaa! You're coming whether you like it or not! I can't go anywhere without you."

Amirah shouted, "Yippee!" and gave her dad a big hug, feeling happy and content.

After a while, Adam asked her.

"By the way, what happened to that girl, Tina, at school? You didn't fill me in on the details yet."

Amirah settled back on her pillow and smiled

gently.

"Yes Dad, there is a bit more of a story there. I'm glad you asked."

Adam finished his tray and put it on the floor and settled back on the pillow next to Amirah, listening intently to what she was saying.

"Go on then," he prompted.

"After Mrs. Jones told her off, her mother came and got her from school. You know Dad, I was a bit afraid when I saw her."

"Why?"

"I don't know, but she is a bit scary."

"What about Tina? Was she afraid?" asked Adam.

"Oh yes, she was terrified, and you know, I felt sorry for her."

"I'll tell you something, Princess, and try to remember it all your life."

"What's that?"

"Every single person in this world has a story to tell. And if people take the time to find out that story, they can usually discover the reasons why people do what they do. Thinking like this makes it easier to forgive," said Adam.

"I don't know much about Tina. Just that her dad left them when she was small and it's only her and her mum at home. She doesn't have any other relatives except some in Perth and they don't see each other much."

"It mustn't be much fun, poor kid."

Amirah started to feel even more sorry for Tina.

"Oh Dad, I'm really glad about what happened then."

"About Mrs. Jones shouting at her?"

"No. Not that Dad. Something else. You see when Tina came to school today her arm was in a sling. She said she sprained it. I don't know how it happened, but anyway, the kids were teasing her, and I just stayed back. I didn't want to get involved in all that mess. By the end of the day, Tina was really upset, and it was raining heavily. I know she has a house key and there is usually no one there for her when she gets home from school. I was feeling a bit sorry for her since the big confrontation. Anyway, I was walking through the playground to go home and there was no one about and then I saw Tina coming up. She was soaking wet because she doesn't have a raincoat and she was carrying her books in one arm and the other arm was in the sling and then she dropped her key."

"You mean her house key?"

"Yes. Right in the middle of a dirty mud puddle."

"Poor kid."

"There was nowhere for her to put her books and her other arm was useless."

"What happened after that?"

"I stood for a while watching her and I remembered what Granny always tells me about the verse in the Qur'an that means if someone does evil to you, you should return it with good then Allah will make you like friends. You know the verse I'm talking about?"

"Yes Princess."

Then Adam recited the verse in Arabic and Amirah listened.

"That's it. Well, Granny's always reminds me of that one."

Adam smiled, "Granny is a treasure huh?"

"Oh yes. Well, I saw Tina standing there helpless and I was about to try to help but then I remembered how awful she has been, and I stopped."

"You didn't!" cried Adam.

He sat up and looked at her seriously.

"Wait. I haven't finished Dad," smiled Amirah. "Then I said *'A`udhubillahi mina ash-shaitanar-Rajeem'* and when I said that my mind felt clear again and I walked up to her."

"What did you say?" asked Adam.

"I said, 'Hi Tina '. Then she nodded. I asked her if that was her house key, and she nodded again. She didn't look at me. So, I just pulled up my sleeves and dug around in that yucky puddle until I found her key. Then I gave it to her and started walking home again."

"Did she say or do anything else?" asked Adam.

"She ran after me and called me."

"What did she call you, 'snowball'?"

"No, not this time Dad," smiled Amirah.

"What did she say?"

"She said 'hey, you wanna' walk a bit'? And I said, 'Okay.' We walked down the street together and didn't talk. When I got to my corner I said, 'See you tomorrow,' and she nodded, and I came home."

"Great," said Adam.

"Is it great Dad? How?"

"I think you've just made a friend."

"I don't think me and Tina will ever be friend friends."

"You keep on being nice to her and you never know how Allah will change people's hearts. Her life has not been very nice until now."

Amirah nodded her head.

"If Allah wants to open the way for someone and bless them, He sends them a good friend and how wonderful it would be if you could be a friend to that girl."

"I'd like that, Dad."

"And try not to keep any ill feelings, Princess. People make dumb mistakes but it's always better to forgive. Afterall, we all need forgiveness."

"Dad, I've found that the more we understand about people, the easier it is to forgive."

"True."

They sat together in silence for a while. Each absorbed in their own thoughts.

"So, when are we going to travel?"

"Well, according to what I found out today, it sounds like we'll be going just after your birthday *Inshallah*. But it may be a bit later. Not sure."

"It will be hard to leave Granny," said Amirah sadly.

Adam laughed. "It will be harder to stop her from coming!"

"You mean Granny is coming to Egypt too?"

"Just try and keep her away!"

Amirah jumped around in happiness.

"I have a feeling that this is going to be a trip to remember!"

Glossary

1. *Allah*: Arabic for God.

1. *Alhamdulillah*: All praise and thanks be to Allah.

2. *Assalam alaikum*: Islamic greeting meaning 'peace be with you'.

3. *A`udhubillahi mina ash-shaitanar-Rajeem*: I seek refuge with Allah from the accursed Satan.

4. Bit of a dip: Go for a swim.

5. Bonkers: To go out of one's mind. A playful term.

6. Chuck me in: To throw me in.

7. Coyotes: A kind of wild dog that is also a character in the cartoon with the 'road runner'. The coyote is a foolish, greedy character that continually tries to catch the road runner but always fails.

8. *Du`aa*: Supplication to Allah, the Almighty.

9. Dumb: Foolish.

10. Freelance: To do contract work for different companies or selling one's work to them.

11. *Hadith*: Sayings and traditions of Prophet Muhammad (peace be upon him).

12. *Inshaa Allah*: If God wills.

13. *Istikharah*: A two *rak`ah* prayer followed by the *du`aa Istikharah* which is performed seeking Allah's guidance when making a decision.

14. *Jazaka Allahu khairan*: 'May Allah bless you.' It is said by someone who is given something, as an alternative to saying thank you.

15. *Jihad*: Any form of legitimate struggle for justice in the cause of Islam.

16. Knap sack: A bag that is carried on one's back and usually used for camping or mountain climbing.

17. Knee high to a grasshopper: A term referring to someone who is very young.

18. Knuckle buster: A ring worn by people who want to fight and hurt their opponents.

19. *Mashaa Allah*: Praising Allah by acknowledging the fact that everything is as He has willed.

20. Milk bar: A corner store.

21. Plonked: To let oneself fall comfortably.

22. *Qibla*: The direction a Muslim faces in prayer.

The Muslim faces towards the *Ka`bah* (Sacred mosque) in Makkah, Saudi Arabia.

23. *Rak`ah*: Unit of prayer.

24. Raining cats and dogs: Raining heavily.

25. Road runner: A cartoon character of a bird that runs so fast on a highway that nothing can ever catch it. It is always being chased by a foolish coyote that continually endangers itself but never catches the road runner.

26. Ruffled: Upset.

27. Scared the daylights out of me: To be extremely frightened.

28. *Shaitan*: Satan.

29. Shelter shed: A building in the school yard that students can use to protect themselves from bad weather during the break at school.

30. *Sujood*: A position in prayer when the forehead is placed on the ground. It is the time of great closeness to Allah, the Almighty.

31. Top it all off: The most important of all.

32. Vegemite: A black, salty spread put on bread and butter.

33. *Walyyak*: 'And the same to you.' It is said as a

reply to *JazakaAllahukhairan*.

34. Wanna': Want to

35. *Waalaikumassalam*: Reply to the above greeting meaning 'And with you be peace.'

36. Weetbix: A brand of cereal eaten with milk and sugar.

37. Wimp: A coward.

38. Wretches: A rascal; an evil character.

39. *Wudu'*: The act of cleansing oneself before prayer.

40. Yep: Yes.

The Colour

of Fear

Amirah is now fourteen years old and she, her dad and Granny are travelling to Egypt, planning to stay for one year. She is growing up and wants more independence, but will her dad trust her? Now an adolescent, Amirah is beginning to understand more about people and life, but she often feels confused. She will have adventures, face challenges, and make important decisions. What choices will she make? Will she face her fears? Where will these choices lead her? What will she learn?